MW01291947

# Secrets of the

# Prayer Shawl

## M.M.Ninan

**Secrets of the Prayer Shawl**

Prof.M.M.Ninan

ISBN 978-0-359-07741-0

90000

9 780359 077410

# Secrets of the Prayer Shawl

## The TALLIT

טלית

**PROF.M.M.NINAN**

# THE SECRETS OF THE PRAYER SHAWL

## PROF. M. M. NINAN

## CONTENTS

**What is a Talit**                                              **1**

    Out of Egypt                              4
    The arba kanfots                          7
    A tallis gadol (Large Tallis)             8
    Chuppah in Weddings                       8
    Covering the Head                         10

**Tzitzit - The Fringe**                                         **11**
    Threads and knots                         17
    Tying the Tzitzit                         20
    Meaning of Tzitzit                        22
    Putting on the Tallit                     26

**Prayer Shawl and Bible Manners and Customs**                   **27**
    The dead are wrapped in it when they are buried.   28
    Proof of Resurrection:                    29
    Prayer Closet                             30
    Ruth And Boaz                             31
    The Hem of His Garment                    34
    The Tzitzit and Jesus                     35
    "Swaying" as You Pray                     36
    Tallit a Kum36

**A Mystical Interpretation of Tzitzit**                         **38**
**Talmudic Sources Concerning Prayer Shawls and Threads**        **45**
**Christian Stola and the Prayer Shawl**                         **49**
    Roman Catholic Church                     50
    Eastern Churches                          52
    Omophorion                                53
    Episcopalian Churches                     54

## What is a tallit?

*The Lord said to Moses as follows:*
*"Speak to the Israelite people and instruct them to make for themselves*
*fringes (Tzitzit) on the corners (Kanphei) of their garments throughout the*
*ages;   let them attach a cord of blue to the fringe at each corner.*
*That shall be your fringe; look at it and recall all the commandments*
*of the Lord and observe them,*
*so that you do not follow your heart and eyes in your lustful urge.*
*Thus you shall be reminded to observe all my commandments*
*and to be holy to your God.*
*I the Lord am your God,*
*who brought you out of the land of Egypt to be your God:*
*I AM, the Lord your God"*
Numbers 15:37-40


*And You shall make tassels on the four corners of the garment*
*with which you cover yourself.*
Deuteronomy 22:12

1

The tallit (Modern Hebrew: טַלִּית) (pronounced TAH-lis in Yiddish) is a prayer shawl. It is a rectangular-shaped piece of linen or wool with special fringes called Tzitzit on each of the four corners. The purpose of the garment is really to hold the Tzitzit.

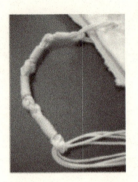

The correct plural of tallit in Modern Hebrew is tallitot, pronounced tah-lee-TOT; the traditional Sephardi plural of tallét is talletot, pronounced tah-leh-TOT,

Most tallitot have a neckband also, called an Atarah, which has the blessing one recites when donning the tallit, embroidered across it. The tallit is prayer shawl which when used to cover the head also creates a personal isolated space for prayer, shutting out the world around you. The name Tallit comes from the two Hebrew words:

## TAL meaning tent

## and

## ITH meaning little.

Thus, you have tallith as a LITTLE TENT. It is this that Jesus was referring to when he said:
Mat 6:6 But when you pray, go into your room and shut the door and pray to your Father who is in secret; and your Father who sees in secret will reward you.

By wrapping yourself in it, or by covering your head with it, you can create an individual tent for yourself to converse with God.

The Tallit bag

The Tallit which can be spread out like a rectangular sheet, is woven of wool or silk, in white, with black or blue stripes at the ends. The tradition is that the tallit is worn only during the morning prayers, except for the Kol Nidre service during Yom Kippur. The garment can be made out of linen, wool, silk or synthetics, so long as the biblical prohibition against the wearing of clothing combining linen and wool is observed.

The Holy One, blessed be, surrounded Israel with the commandment of:
tephillin for their heads,
tephillin for their arms,
tzitzit for their clothing and
mezuzot for their doors.
[Talmud Menachot 43a-b]

## Out of Egypt

Egypt is a hot country with very little rain and little cold to worry about. So ancient Egyptians wore as little as possible due to the heat. Ordinary people wore nothing but a loin cloth to cover nakedness. Noblemen would occasionally wear tunics, cloaks, or robes, though. Women, who mostly stayed indoors, would likewise wear little clothing, though they used elaborate jewelleries. Men also shaved off their head to reduce heat.

Egyptian dresses.

Into this culture came Jacob and his clan of 70 people with their beards and thick hair and covering the entire body with wool and linen. Midrash tells us that they observed the laws of tzniut — the laws of modesty. They continued to wear their traditional dress of nomads even in Egypt. It was their distinct culture that kept them as a separate people which eventually led to their liberation and return to Canaan. Without that they would have just merged with the Egyptians and lost as an ethnic identity.

## The dress of the nomads

The original tallit probably resembled the "'abayah," or blanket, worn by the Bedouins for protection from sun and rain, and which has black stripes at the ends. It usually had tassels also. Thus the shawl covering the top part of the body was the normal dress of the Jews as they came out of Egypt and suited well for their wilderness journey.

**Roman Toga**

Roman toga was also very similar. The toga was a distinctive garment of Ancient Rome. It consisted of a long sash of cloth, of over 6 meters in length. This sash was wrapped around the body loosely and was generally worn over a tunic. The toga was made of wool, and the tunic underneath was made of linen.

Women's dress consisted of:
TUNICA (under dress),STOLA (overdress), and PALLA (wrap).
Menachot 43a say: "All must observe the law of tzitzit, Cohanim,
Levites and Israelites, converts, women and slaves."   But women
are not to be obligated to wear a tallit.

Num 15:38 "Speak to the people of Israel, and bid them to make
tassels on the corners of their garments throughout their
generations, and to put upon the tassel of each corner a cord of
blue.

What was distinctive to the new commandment was not the regular
tassels at the ends but the tassels at the four corners of the
rectangular shawl.

The Torah explicitly commands that Tzitzit be added to the four
corners of garments (Maimonides considered it one of the most
important of the 613 Mitzvot); traditionally the wearing of Tzitzit
began with this commandment, though biblical scholars consider it
to be much older, and argue that the commandment reflected an
already existing practice. If this is true the distinctiveness is simply
the association of the Tzitzit with the 613 Mitzovot.

Tzitzit (Ashkenazi pronunciation: tzitzis) are fringes or tassles
(Hebrew: x-m (Biblical), X'!'J'| (Mishnaic)) found on a tallit worn by
observant Jews as part of practicing Judaism. In Orthodox Judaism
it is only worn by males;

## The arba kanfots
After the 13th century AD, when the dressing styles of the nations
where the Jews were in dispersion changed, Tzitzit began to be
worn on new inner garments, known as Arba Kanfos, rather than
the outer garments. This inner garment was a 3ft by 1ft rectangle,

with a hole in the centre for the head to pass through; the modern.
it was worn just under the overcoat but over the inner dress. These
arba kanfots constantly reminds the wearer that they are under
the law and protected by divine law.

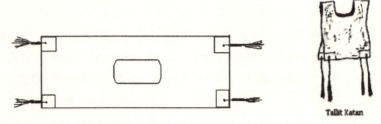

Tallit Katan

## A tallis gadol (Large Tallis)

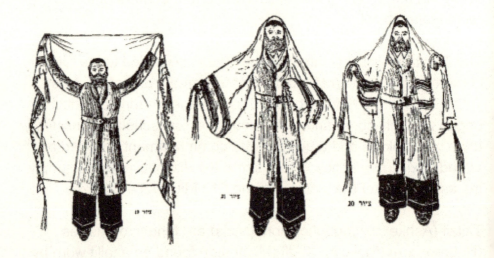

A tallis gadol is much bigger.

## Chuppah in Weddings

A chuppah, a piece of cloth held up by four poles, serves as a
marriage canopy in traditional Jewish wedding ceremonies. The
bride and groom stand under the chuppah during the ceremony.

The canopy symbolizes the new home being created by the couple. Some people use a tallit tor the chuppah cloth. The chuppah is usually held outside, under the stars, just prior to sundown, as a reminder of the blessing given by God to Abraham, that his children will be as numerous "as the stars of the heavens."
A tallit is commonly spead over the wedding symbolizing the unity of husband and wife and reminding them of the commandment

Gen 2:24 Therefore a man leaves his father and his mother and cleaves to his wife, and they become one flesh

"Bless Adonai, O my soul. Adonai, My God, You are very great, You are clothed in glory and majesty. You have wrapped yourself with a garment of light, spreading out the heavens like a curtain.":

The mystical interpretation of the covering shawl is the representation of the covering of glory of God on man.

And Jesus' high priestly prayer was:
John 17:22 And the glory which thou gavest me I have given them; that they may be one, even as we are one:

Joh 17:21 that they may all be one; even as thou, Father, art in me, and I in thee, that they also may be in us.

It is this triple order of oneness that is represented in the Tallit covering. it is this order of oneness that is represented by the chuppa the covering and also the Tallit when used in prayer.
In the traditional prayer book the following meditation before putting on the tallit is found, based on the Kabbalah:

"I am here enwrapping myself in thisfringed robe, in fulfillment of the command of my Creator, as it is written in the Torah, they shall make them a fringe upon the comers of their garments throughout their generations. And even as I cover myself with the tallit in this world, so may my soul deserve to be clothed with a beauteous spiritual robe in the World to Come, in the garden of Eden." .

## Covering the Head

The ultra-Orthodox wear the tallit over the head when they recite the more important prayers. The earlier authorities are divided on the question of covering the head. Some are none too happy with a practice that might be seen as showing off, since the essential idea of covering the head in this way is for the worshipper to be lost in concentration, on his own before God, as it were. Religious one-upmanship is generally frowned upon. Some hold that only a talmid hakham, a man learned in the Torah, should cover his head with the tallit. The final ruling is that one should follow whatever is the local custom.

## Must be made of one material

There are very few religious requirements with regard to the design of the tallit. The tallit must be long enough to be worn over the shoulders (as a shawl), not just around the neck (as a scarf), to fulfill the requirement that the tzitzis be on a "garment." It may be made of any material, but must not be made of a combination of wool and linen, because that combination is forbidden on any clothing. (Lev. 19:19; Deut. 22:11)

Deu 22:11 You shall not wear a mingled stutt, wool and linen Together.
This may be because the shawl represents ONENESS ot the cosmos within ONE God.

## Tzitzit - The Fringe
The Lord said to Moses as follows: Speak to the Israelite people and instruct them to make for themselves fringes (Tzitzit) on the corners (Kanphei) כנפי of their garments throughout the ages; letthem attach a cord of blue to the fringe at each corner. That shall be your fringe; look at it and recall all the commandments of the Lord and observe them, so that you do not follow your heart and eyes in your lustful urge. Thus you shall be reminded to observe all my commandments and to be holy to your God. I the Lord am your God, who brought you out of the land of Egypt to be your God: I, the Lord your God
Numbers 15:37-40
and
You shall make tassels on the four corners of the garment with which you cover yourself.
Deuteronomy 22:12

The reason tor the tassels is given by the torah.

The sole significance of the tallit was in the tzitzit.

עִבְרִית לַנּוֹצְרִים

וְהָיָה לָכֶם לְצִיצִת וּרְאִיתֶם אֹתוֹ וּזְכַרְתֶּם אֶת־כָּל־מִצְוֹת יְהוָה וַעֲשִׂיתֶם
אֹתָם וְלֹא־תָתֻרוּ אַחֲרֵי לְבַבְכֶם וְאַחֲרֵי עֵינֵיכֶם אֲשֶׁר־אַתֶּם זֹנִים אַחֲרֵיהֶם׃

And it shall be a tassel for you to look at and remember all the commandments of the LORD, to do them, not to follow after your own heart and your own eyes, which you are inclined to whore after. - Numbers 15:39

The term Tzitzith recalls the tzitz, the golden plate, worn by the high priest, upon which were engraved the words "Holy unto God" (Exodus 28:36). Just as tzitz is derived from my (to gaze; ct. Song 2:9), because it was worn on the forehead, a place visible to all (Rashbam), - Tzitzith, too, is derived from the same root.

Tzitzith also refers to the hairs, or "fringes" on the forehead (cf. Ezek. 8:3). This word thus denotes that the fringes are to be seen, to be looked upon, and its best translation is, therefore, "show-fringes" thus the fringes are attached to the garment in order to be seen. It is a mnemonic device.

**Fringe as Identification**
The use of fringes itself was not new.
Assyrians and Babylonians wore fringes and they believed that fringes assured the wearer of the protection of the gods. So it is an age old mnemonic technique.

This ornate hem from where the fringes started, was a "symbolic extension of the owner and more specifically of the owner's rank and authority." In all societies and cultures the fringes were the "ID. of nobility."

In Mari, an ancient city in what is now Syria, a professional prophet or diviner would enclose with his report to the King a lock of his hair and a piece of his hem....Sometimes the hem was impressed on a clay tablet as a kind of signature.

Requests accompanied by grasping the fringes of the one from whom you wanted something could not be refused.

Exorcists used the hem of a patient's garment in their healing ceremonies.

A husband could divorce his wife by cutting off the hem of his wife's robe.

Professor Milgrom of Berkeley University, who write one of the critical volumes of commentary on the Torah for the Jewish Publication Society, saw the tzitzit as a sign of royalty or the priesthood. They were worn on the lower hem of the robe, and thus signifying those who are called out as a nation as a "kingdom of priests"

The Jewish prayer shawl displayed a person's authority. The more important the person, the more elaborate his prayer shawl. In the period of Kings, a Prophets would cut of one of their tassels to send along with their prophecy to ensure the king it was their prophecy. In 1 Samuel 15:27-29, Saul tore Samuel's tassel from his shawl. Samuel told Saul the kingdom of Israel would be torn from him as Saul had torn Samuel's tassel (authority) from him. We also see David's anguish in 1 Samuel 24:5 when he cut the tassel from Saul's shawl. David knew he was to replace Saul as king over Israel, but, by cutting the tassel off Saul's shawl, he had gotten ahead of God's timing. Thus, stripping Saul of his authority by cutting off Saul's tassel, David repented before God and Saul in 1 Samuel 24:5.

## Why do tallit have blue or black stripes?

The reason why the tallis is striped is simply because that was the fashion in Greece and Rome. But this doesn't answer the question of why blue or black? Tzitzis are supposed to include a thread of blue wool in each tassle. The stripes on the tallit remind us of the 'strand of techelet' once worn as part of the tzitzit. The Torah commands that tzitzis contain a thread of Tichales (blue). The reason for this is contained in Sotah 17b.

Blue is like sea,
Sea is like sky
Sky is like the Throne of the Lord.

### Royal Blue

in each tassel was to be one wool thread dyed in blue. Aaron, the High Priest of Israel, had his robe dyed in purple as recorded in Exodus 28:31-35.

The color is still known as "royal" blue. By placing one blue thread in every man's prayer shawl, God identified every Jewish man as king in his home. The fact that each man was allowed to mix linen with wool in his tassel also reveals how God identified each man as a priest. This combination was reserved only for the priests. The Torah only calls for a few blue threads, one for each fringe, perhaps because that meant that even the poorest Israelite could afford them.

This color Royal Blue was used in the ecclesiastical authority and in the temple where authority was involved. Thus we see them in:

- **Curtains of the tabernacle.**
Exo 26:1 "Moreover you shall make the tabernacle with ten curtains of fine twined linen and blue and purple and scarlet stuff "

- **The veil of the ark.**
Exo 26:31 "And you shall make a veil of blue and purple and scarlet stuff and fine twined linen

- **The screen of the door of the Tent of Meeting .**
Exo 26:36 "And you shall make a screen for the door of the tent, of blue and purple and scarlet stuff and fine twined linen, embroidered with needlework.

- **The Ephod of the Priest**
Exo 28:6 And they shall make the ephod of gold, of blue and purple and scarlet stuff, and of fine twined linen, skilfully Worked

- **Headdress of the Priest**
Exo 28:37 And you shall fasten it on the turban by a lace of blue; it shall be on the front of the turban.

- **girdle of the Priest**
Exo 39:29 and the girdle of fine twined linen and of blue and purple and scarlet stuff, embroidered with needlework; Thus it is evident that the significance of the blue thread in the fringe implies the calling of the Jews:

15

Exo 19:5-6 Now therefore, if you will obey my voice and keep my covenant, you shall be my own possession among all peoples; for all the earth is mine, and you shall be to me a kingdom of priests and a holy nation. These are the words which you shall speak to the children of Israel."

The Tzitzit is thus a constant reminder to this great responsibility. Being surrounded by the Mitzvot of Phylacteries, Tzitzit-Fringes and Mezuzot guarantees protection against Sinning: Menachot 43b Karaite Tzitzit, using a generic blue dye.

According to the Talmud, tekhelet (תכלת) which appears 48 times inthe Tanach. This is translated by the Septuagint as "iakinthos"(blue). This is a specific dye of blue produced from a creaturereferred to as a "chillazon" impying that no other blue dyes areacceptable (Tosefta). The Talmud recounts that the Chilazone

appears only once in seventy years (Menachot 44a).

> **Chilazon:** Its dye is used for the Techelet Dye for Tzitzit-
> Fringes: Menachot 44a
> A description of its appearance: Menachot 44a
> It is only found once in 70 years: Menachot 44a
> The Chilazon was found in Zevulun's portion in Israel:
> Megillah6a

Sometime following the Talmudic era (500-600 CE) the industry which produced this dye was destroyed - R. Herzog attributes the demise of the industry to the Arab conquest in 638. It became rarer and rarer. Over time the Jewish community even lost the tradition of which creature is known as "the hillazon" that produced this dye. Hence, the 'strand of techelet' became a mitzvah which no jew was able to fulfill. Since the source of the dye was lost, Jews left the stand un-dyed wearing plain white tzitzit without any dyes. Some substituted the blue with the black stripes found on many traditional tallitot as representing the loss of this dye. Karaites, who reject the Oral Law maintain that any blue dye may be used.

In the late 19th century a chassidic Rebbe, Rabbi Gershon Henoch Leiner, devoted himself to rediscovering the correct species and dye making process. He concluded that the chilazon is sepia officinalis, the common cuttlefish. In 1889 he reenacted the making of the blue, techeiles, dye, and many thousands of chassidim began to wear it. In the early 20th century, Rabbi Yitzchak HaLevi Herzog studied the subject and came to a different conclusion, believing that the lost chilazon was really from the Janthina species of snail.

## Threads and knots

The fringe (tzitzit) on each corner is made of four strands, each of which is made of eight fine threads (known as kafulshemoneh). The four strands are passed through a hole (or according to some: two holes) 1-2 inches (25 to 50 mm) away from the corner of the Cloth

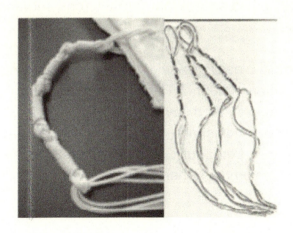

The tzitzis strings of one corner of a tallit. Note how the eight strings are really four that are folded through the hole on the tallit. There are numerous customs as to how to tie the fringe. The Talmud explains that the Bible requires an upper knot (kesher e/yon) and one wrapping of three winds (hulya). The Talmud goes on to explain that the Rabbis enjoined that between 7 to 13 hulyot be tied, and that the initial and final winds must be the color of the garment, the interving ones being the color tekhelet. As for the making of knots in between the hulyot, the Talmud is inconclusive, and as such poskim throughout the ages have varyingly interpreted this requirement. The Talmud described tying assuming the use of tekhelet, however, following the loss of the source of the dye, various customs of tying were introduced to compensate for the lack of this primary element.

**Tzitzit, with a thread of tekhelet**
Though many methods have been proposed the one that gained the widest acceptance can be described as follows:

The four strands are put through the hole in the corner of the garment, thus making two sets of four threads (one set on each side of the hole).

Before tying begins, a blessing is said: L'Shem Mitzvot Tzitzit (For the sake of the Commandment of Tzitzit). Some Rabbis are of the opinion that one should instead say Baruch atah Adonai Elohainu Melech HaOlam, asher kiddishanu b'mitzvotav v'tzivanu la'asot tzitzit (Blessed are you, Lord, our God, king of the universe who sanctified us with His commandments and commanded us to make tzitzit).

The two sets of stands are knotted together twice, and then the "shamash" (a longer strand) is wound around the remaining seven strands a number of times (see below). The two sets are then knotted again twice. This procedure is repeated three times. A commonly formed pattern of windings is 7-8-11-13 (totalling 39 winds - the gematria of the "God is One"). Others, especially Sephardim, have 10 and 5 and 6 and 5, a combination that

represents directly the spelling of the Tetragrammaton.
Rashi, a prominent Jewish commentator, bases the number of knots on a gematria: the word tzitzit (in its Mishnaic spelling) has the value 600. Each tassel has eight threads (when doubled over) and five sets of knots, totalling 13. The sum of all numbers is 613, traditionally the number of mitzvot (commandments) in the Torah. This reflects the concept that donning a garment with tzitzit reminds its wearer of all Torah commandments.

# Tying the Tzitzit

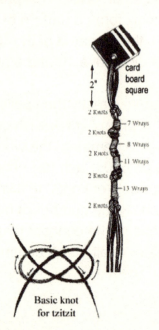

Tying Tzitzit is a Jewish art, a form of macrame.

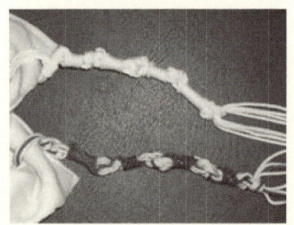

The comparison of the **Ashkenaz**i and the **Shephardi** style. Note the difference in the number and the style of windings

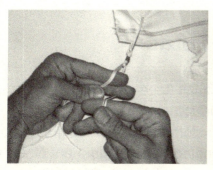

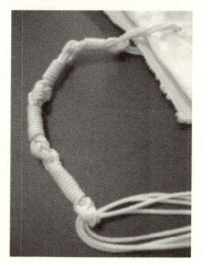

The tzitzis strings of one corner of a tallit. Theeight strings are really four that are foldedthrough the hole on the tallit. This tzitzit is tied in Ashkenazi—style.

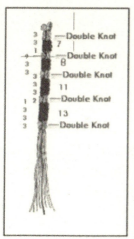
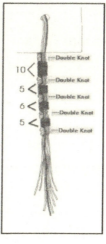

How to tie the Shephardic and Chasidic knots.

# Meaning of Tzitzit

The significant part of the tallit is the Tzitzit (tzee-tzeet) [tassels, also called fringes] attached to the four corners of the rectangular cloth. The design on the cloth, and the cloth itself, have no great significance. Any tassels or strings hanging from the garment other than those at the four corners are also insignificant and are for aesthetics only. The Tzitzit are what makes this garment a religious object.

There are a number of symbolism in the knots and windings

1. The five knots tied in each tassel can be viewed as symbolic of the five Books of Moses, these books are known as Genesis, Exodus, Leviticus, Numbers, and Deuteronomy. This is the material written in the Sefer Torah [Torah scroll]. Of course, the Torah is the foundation for all of Judaism.

The knots and windings are also considered symbolic of the Shema (shem-ah):

שמע ישראל יהוה אלוהינו יהוה אחד

Shema Yisrael Adonai Elohenu Adonai Echad --
Hear Oh Israel, the Lord is our God, the Lord is One
[Deuteronomy 6:4].

[In prayers, "Israel" refers to the Jewish people. It is short for "Children of Israel." "Eretz Yisrael" the "Land of Israel" ] The Shema is commonly referred to as the watchword of the Jewish faith. The recitation of this line is a important part of the morning and evening services.

22

2. The five knots can be viewed as representing the first five (Hebrew) words of the Shema. The last word, Echad, is represented by the windings between the knots. Echad means "one." The windings bind the knots into a single unit.

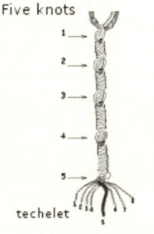

Five knots

techelet

Eight Threads

3. Each Tzitzit is made from 8 strings, 7 white and one blue. 'Seven' is the number representing perfection in the physical realm. 'Eight', therefore, transcends the physical realm and symbolizes a direct link to the spiritual realm.

Each group of 8 strings is knotted 5 times to form a Tzitzit. There are five books in the Torah.

Each of the 4 tzitzit have 8 strings, making a total of 32 strings. Thirty-two is the numeric value of the Hebrew word for "HEART". The tzitzit's loose strings represent God's 'heart strings'.

613 mitzvot (or 613 Commandments. Hebrew: תרי"ג מצוות transliterated as Taryag mitzvot; TaRYaG is the acronym for the numeric value of "613".) In Judaism there is a tradition that the Torah (i.e. the "Pentateuch") contains 613 mitzvot (mitzvot in Hebrew means "commandments", from mitzvah - "precept", plural: mitzvot; from, tzavah- "command").

According to the main source, of these 613 commandments, 248 are mitzvot aseh ("positive commandments") and 365 are mitzvot lo

23

taaseh ("negative commandments"). 365 corresponded to the number of days in a solar year and 248 wasat that time believed to be the number ofbones or significant organs in the human body.

**4. "Two-House" tzit-tzit.**
Consists of 12 strings (6 for Judah & 6 for Ephraim). All strings begin woven together into 7 braids, representing the unified House. The Houses are then split, again with 7 braids each. The two Houses are then woven back together again into 7 braids representing the re-unification of the two Houses.

# Putting on the Tallit

## Putting on a Tallit Katan

The tzitzit are first inspected to make sure they are properly intact before wearing the tallit katan. While holding the tallit katan, in readiness to put it on, the following blessing is recited. (if the person will later put on a tallit gadol, this blessing is omitted.)
mix nim 'w nixi |']1IXYJ1|JEl'l|7 wum n'1|un Tm n'n'm 3 mm qnn
Barukh atah, adonai, eloheinu, melech haolam, asher kiedshanu b'mitzvotav, v'tzievahnu al mitzvat tzitzit

Blessed are You, Lord, our God, King of the universe, Who has sanctified us with His commandments, and commanded us regarding the commandment of fringes

ברוך אתה ה׳ אלהינו מלך העולם אשר קדשנו במצותיו וצונו על מצות ציצת
*Barukh atah, adonai, eloheinu, melech haolam, asher kiedshanu
b'mitzvotav, v'tzievahnu al mitzvat tzitzit
Blessed are You, Lord, our God, King of the universe, Who has
sanctified us with His commandments, and commanded us
regarding the commandment of fringes*
After donning the tallit katan, many kiss the tziztit; some add the following:

יהי רצון מלפניך ה׳ אלהי ואלהי אבותי שתהי חשובה מצות ציצת לפניך כאלו
קימתיה בכל פרטיה ודקדוקי וכונותיה ותריג מצות התלוים בה אמן סלה
*Y'hie rahtzon miel'fanehchah, adonai ehlohay vaylohay ahvotay,
sheht'hay khashuvah mitzvot tzitzit lfahnehkhah, k'ielu
kieyahm'tieah b'khal prahtehyah v'diek'dukehyah v'khahu'notehyeh,
v'tahr'yag mitzvot hat'luyim ba. Amen Selah*

May it be the will before you, Lord, my God and the God of my forefathers, that it should be considered the commandment of fringes before You as if I had fullfiled it in all its aspects, its details and its intentions, as well as the 613 commandments that are dependent on it. So be it, [consider what we have said].

**Kissing the tzitzit**

There are several times during the sen/ice when people kiss the tzitzit symbolically.

First is during the recitation of the third paragraph of the Shema (Numbers 15:37-41) which mentions the tzitzit three times. As the worshiper reads the word "tzitzit," it is customary to kiss the tzitzit, which were gathered together in one hand prior to reciting the Shema.

When the Torah is removed from the Ark and carried around the synagogue in a Hakatah (procession), those within reach touch the Torah mantle with tzitzit (if they are wearing a tallit) or a siddur (prayerbook) it they are not. They then kiss the tzitzit or siddur which touched the Torah scroll.

# Prayer Shawl
# and
# Bible Manners and Customs

The Prayer Shawl, (aka. tallis, tallit, talis) is a religious symbol, a garment, shroud, canopy, cloak which envelops the Jew both physically and spiritually, in prayer and celebration, in joy and sorrow.

While some other Jewish garments or objects might be treated more casually, the tallit is a special personal effect, generally used for many years or a lifetime and never discarded. Most Jewish men (and some women) own very few tallitot in their lifetimes. A threadbare tallit is treated with great respect, as if it had a mantle of holiness, acquired from years of use. Although there is no mandatory tradition, in Conservative, reform, and otherwise non-religious families a tallit, as well as tefillin, is likely to be given as a special gift, from father to son, from father-in-law to son-in-law, or from teacher to student. It might be purchased to mark a special occasion, such as a wedding, a bar/bat mitzvah, or a trip to Israel. When a man dies, it is traditional that he be buried dressed only in his kittel, with his tallit is draped over him.

Anyone attending an orthodox synagogue today will see that the men are all wearing prayer shawls. It is a very important part of Jewish life. Learning about this sacred garment will teach many exciting lessons from other Bible stories, even in the New Testament!

It is used at all major Jewish occasions: circumcisions, bar mitsvahs, weddings and burials. It protects the scrolls of the Torah when they are moved.

27

When a child fall sick, the parents would wrap the child in a tallit on the floor and pace the floor around the child praying for the healing of the child.

It inspired the Jewish flag.
Three separate people had the same idea.
They just unfurled the prayer shawl and added the Shield of David and created the flag of Israel.

## The dead are wrapped in it when they are buried.

### Burial

After death, Jews are buried with varying customs, depending on where they are to be buried. In the Diaspora, burial takes place within a plain, wooden casket. The corpse is collected from the place of death (home, hospital, etc.) by the chevra kadisha (burial committee). After a ritual washing of the body , the body is dressed in a kittel (shroud) and then a tallit. One of the tzitzit is then cut off and laid atop the rest of the tallit. In the Land of Israel, burial is without a casket, and the kittel and tallith are the only coverings for the corpse.

The Yemen Jews have a practice of wearing an all black tallit at prayer during a period of mourning.
Some Jews have an all white tallit worn on Yom Kippur, symbolizing rebirth.

In addition to tahrihim, the shroud, some Jews are wrapped in the prayer shawl (tallit) in which they prayed. Every tallit is tied with four sets of knotted fringes (tzizit), which symbolize the commandment (mitzvot) incumbent upon Jews. Before the tal/itis placed on a body for burial, however, one of the sets of fringes is cut to demonstrate that the person is no longer bound by the religious obligations of the living.

## Proof of Resurrection:
### Jesus folded his Tallit when he arose from the dead.

Yeshua, the Messiah, also was put in the tomb with His prayer shawl about His head as was the custom of burial. The TALLIT, which the KJV Holy Bible calls the napkin, is one of the many great infallible proofs, as Jesus showed Himself ALIVE after his death on the cross.

John 20:6-8 we read, "Then cometh Simon Peter following him, and went into the sepulchre, and seeth the linen clothes lie, And the napkin, that was about his head, not lying with the linen clothes, but wrapped together in a place by itself. Then went in also that other disciple, which came first to the sepulchre, and he saw, and believed."

As Peter and then John entered the empty tomb, they saw something that immediately convinced them that the resurrection of

Yeshua was irrefutable fact. This is just a single small example of the richness of the proof of the resurrection. It also shows why Gentiles should rejoice that the Jewish Roots of the Gospel are being restored by the modern Messianic movement.

Yeshua knew that when Simon Peter burst into the tomb and found it empty, Peter would think the Romans had somehow disposed of the body. That is why Yeshua, at the time of His resurrection, on Saturday, the Sabbath, Nissan 17, three days and nights after His death on the cross on Wednesday, Nissan 14, 30AD, folded His Tallit. Yeshua took the time to precisely fold His prayer shawl, His TALLIT, and lay it apart from the other grave wrappings.

When Peter saw the tallit, as only Yeshua would fold it, he knew that the Romans did not take the body; because, if they had, NO WAY would they have folded, or even known how Yeshua folded His tallit. Yeshua MUST be alive to fold that tallit, Yeshua's way, as Peter and John knew very well.

## Prayer Closet

TALITH contains two Hebrew words;
TAL .meaning tent and ITH meaning little.
Thus, you have LITTLE TENT. Each man had his own little tent. Six million Jews could not fit into the tent of meeting that was set up in the Old Testament. Therefore, what was given to , them was their own private sanctuary where they could meet with God. Each man had one! His Prayer Shawl or Talith. They would pull it up over their head, forming a tent, where they would begin to chant and sing their Hebrew songs, and call upon God. It was intimate, private, and set apart from anyone else -- enabling them to totally focus upon God. This was their prayer closet!

Matthew 6:6 tells us to enter into our "closet" for prayer. When a Jewish man puts on his prayer shawl, he closes himself in and shuts out the world. This effectively becomes his "prayer closet" and this was an image in the mind of Matthew when he wrote the admonition of Jesus.

## Ruth And Boaz

Jewish weddings are sometimes performed under a prayer shawl held up during the ceremony by four poles called a chupa or huppah. In Mid East culture they cast a garment over one being claimed for marriage. In Numbers 15:38 the word translated border or corner is a Hebrew word which can also be translated wings as it is some seventy-six times in the biblical text.

For this reason, the corners of the prayer shawl are often called wings.

Lord speaks to Jerusalem

Ezekiel 16:8, , "and I spread my wing over thee, and covered thy nakedness,"

Psalm 91 "abide under the shadow of the Almighty " and "under His wings."

In the book of Ruth, Ruth found herself at the feet of Boaz.

According to the Levirate system Ruth was expected to get children to keep her husband's family through the kinsmen of her husband, this move was too fast for Boaz. This was a direct claim for that right from Ruth.

Ruth 3:9 He said, "Who are you?" And she answered, "I am Ruth, your maidservant; spread your skirt over your maidservant, for you are next of kin."

She had the right to be covered by her Jewish spouses Talis as a symbolic expression of marriage symbol. Ruth was also indicating that it was her legal right in accordance with the commandments which the Tiztzit reminded. She was taking the cover of the law of Moses.

Deu 25:5 "If brothers dwell together, and one of them dies and has no son, the wife of the dead shall not be married outside the family to a stranger; her husband's brother shall go in to her, and take her as his wife, and perform the duty of a husband's brother to her.

It is interesting to note that a similar custom still prevails at an orthodox Jewish wedding, when the bridegroom covers his bride with his tallit, his prayer shawl, with its tassels at each corner, signifying that he is taking her into his care.

The hem of a Jew's garment was not, as in modern clothes, a simple fold of the cloth, sewn down to prevent the edge from fraying. It was a decorative feature that made a statement about the status and importance of the wearer. The people of other nearby nations also had this custom. in texts found in Mesopotamia, references indicate that the removal of the fringe of a man's garment was the equivalent of removing part of his personality. To cut off the hem of a wife's garment was regarded as divorcing her. Tablets have been found with the impression of a fringe as the mark of the individual, a personal seal or signature.

In New Testament times, ordinary people only wore a tallit on special occasions, if at all. It was the Pharisees who seem to have worn it regularly and, apparently in some cases, often for show. Jesus expresses no disapproval of the custom itself but he does condemn the extra long fringes that they affected to display their piety [Matthew 23:5]. Thus the hem or fringe of a garment indicated the rank or personality of the wearer.

When David spared Saul's life, he took away evidence that he had him in his power: "Then David arose, and cut off the skirt (hem) of Saul's robe privily," 1 Samuel 24:4.

Why did David do this, and why did his conscience smite him for having done it? Was there some special significance in what he had done? In fact the act of cutting off the skirt (fringe) of Saul's robe was of very great significance, which Saul was not slow to recognize. When the shouting began next day Saul said: "And now, behold, I know well that thou shalt surely be king, and that the kingdom of Israel shall be established in thine hand" (1 Sam. 24:20). David had robbed Saul of his status symbol, the fringe of his robe that identified him as king. The fringes on the garment were a status symbol.

The Prophet Elijah passed his mantle on to Elisha in II Kings 2. Many believe that this mantle was actually his Talis and was symbolic of the power of prayer that Elijah had saturated that mantle with. This mantle that Elijah left behind as he was taken up by a whirlwind into heaven, was what Elisha struck and parted the waters with. Elijah's mantle was a status symbol.

It will be remembered that Jesus castigated the Pharisees for enlarging their fringes (Matt. 23:5), the inference being that they were thereby trying to magnify their importance. Despite this, he must sometimes have worn one himself as the story of the woman who touched the hem of his garment suggests [Luke 8:43, 44]. What was the significance of the hem of His garment and how did she know touching it would heal her? Other people, too, were healed by touching the borders or tassels of his clothes [Mark 6:56].

### The Hem of His Garment
"But unto you that fear my name shall the Sun of righteousness arise with healing in his wings," Malachi 4:2. One of the best known miracles of healing that Jesus performed was the occasion when a woman who had suffered from a hemorrhage for twelve years came up behind him and touched the hem of his garment, Matthew 9:20 The woman was, in fact, reaching for the tassels on Jesus' prayer shawl. In Hebrew, these tassels, which are attached to the corners of the prayer shawl, are called tzitzit. Why should she stoop to touch the fringe? Why not his arm, or his feet?

As the torah was placed over the head, it formed his own tent. WINGS of the garment were formed when the arms were held out. For this reason, the corners of the prayer shawl are often called "wings." During the first century there were several traditions associated with the tzitzit concerning Messiah. One was that these knotted fringes possessed healing powers. Certainly the woman with the issue of blood knew of these traditions, which would explain why she sought to touch the hem (the wings) of Jesus' prayer garment. The same word used in Numbers 15:38 for corner is used in Malachi 4:2 for wings. With this understanding in mind, an ancient Jew under the prayer shawl could be said to be dwelling in the secret place of the Most High and under His wings (Ps.91 :1-4). The lady with the issue knew that if Jesus were the promised Messiah, there would be healing in His wings (fringes). That this was the opinion of many other people is revealed by the crowd who sought his healing powers, "that they might only touch the hem of his garment: and as many as touched were made perfectly whole," Matthew 14:36.

## The Tzitzit and Jesus

In Jesus' day, Jewish men wore a simple tunic both at home and at work. When appearing in public, they would cover their tunic with a large rectangular cloth which draped over the shoulder and fell to the ankles. This cloth was called a tallit and served as protection from cold and rain. Hanging from the end of each of its four corners (wings) was a tzitzit in obedience to the biblical command.

Through the centuries, during times of persecution, Jews were often forbidden to wear the tzitzit on the outside of their garments. This forced them to wear a small four-cornered tallit under their shirts. Today the prayer shawl is called a tallit.

During the first century there were several traditions associated with the tzitzit concerning Messiah. One was that these knotted fringes possessed healing powers. This tradition has its roots in the prophecy of Malachi 4:2 where the Messiah is said to be coming with healing in His wings.

Certainly the woman with the issue of blood knew of these traditions, which would explain why she sought to touch the corner (the wings) of Jesus' prayer garment.

35

The same word used in Numbers 15:38 for corner is used in Malachi 4:2 for wings. With this understanding in mind, an ancient Jew under the prayer shawl could be said to be dwelling in the secret place of the Most High and under His wings (Ps. 91 :1-4). When one realized the significance of this concept to the first-century Hebraic mind, it becomes clear why this woman was instantly healed. She was expressing her faith in Jesus as the Son of Righteousness with healing in His wings and declaring her faith in God's prophetic Word.

## "Swaying" as You Pray

When a Jewish man prays, he sways. Among the reasons offered to explain this moving of the body while praying, two are more widely held. The first comes from Proverbs 20:27, which says, "The lamp of the Lord searches the spirit of a man; it searches out his inmost being". The Jews conclude that the spirit of the man is the candle of the Lord and it should flicker and wave in harmony with the light of the Torah. The second comes from Psalm 35:10, which says, "My whole being will exclaim, 'Who is like you, O Lord?'" This act of swaying produces a trance in which the person thinks only of the Lord as he prays the Word of God. The Apostle Paul speaks of this in Acts 22:17 when he says, "When I returned to Jerusalem and was praying at the Temple, I fell into a trance and saw the Lord speaking". Peter had a similar experience in prayer recorded in Acts 10:9-16. Peter was accustomed to praying three times daily in this manner. This was his afternoon prayer (Mincha). He obviously fell into this trance.

## Tallit a Kum

Another story unfolds in Matthew in Matthew 9:18-26 and Mark 5:20-43. We find Jesus being sent for by Jairus, a ruler of a synagogue, to minister healing to his daughter. Before Jesus can get to her a woman with an issue of blood comes and touches his garment. if she can just touch the "hem of his garment" she will be made whole. The word, translated hem in this passage, is the same one translated as fringes in other passages. She knew that if she could just get hold of God, she could be healed. Jesus knew that He had been touched. Mark 5:30 says Jesus knew virtue went out of him. The word rendered virtue is more accurately translated "power". The Hebrew equivalent from the LXX, is "army or host". Power left Him ........ ..was it power to heal? Yes, to a point, but it was more than that. Cleanliness left Him. The woman rendered Him unclean by touching His clothes. Through no fault of His own, He became unclean and He felt the power leaving Him. This is important to the rest of the story. It was forbidden for a rabbi or priest to touch a dead body and remove his state of cleanliness. When Jesus reached Jairus house, He was told that the girl was dead. Jesus states the she is only asleep and they laugh Him to scorn, Mark 5:40. Why did He make this statement? He wanted them to know she was dead and He was going in. He was allowed to enter because the woman with the issue of blood rendered Him unclean. Then Jesus calls "Talitha Cumi". The translators tell us it means "damsel, arise". There are other words that would have been used to address the girl. What Jesus actually said was more like — Girl in the Tallit, God says arise! This is why He said not to tell what had happened. The people knew she was dead and would just as surely know she was now alive. What Jesus did not want them to know as yet was the tact that He walked, lived and functioned on earth as God and in fact was God! He knew it and those in the room knew it, but He did not want anyone else to know it as yet.

|+++>"

# A MYSTICAL INTERPRETATION OF TZITZIT
## By Yechezkel Gold
http://www.jewishmag.com/30mag/tzitzit/tzitzit.htm

The Torah says that we must make for ourselves fringes (tzitzit) on the corners of our garments (Numbers 15).The Code of Jewish Law, the Shulchan Aruch, explains that a man wearing a garment with four or more corners must tie the tzitzit on the four most distant corners of the garment.

A corner is the meeting point of two edges of the garment, each edge running in a different direction from the one it meets. That is, a corner is a point where two edges no longer can continue on their own separate paths, but rather each limits the other, thereby forming a corner, an area which comes to a point. Like an edge, a corner is an interface of the material and the area of non-material, but unlike the edge which forms a line, a corner is an area which comes to a point.

While checking the fringes before donning the tallit, we say: "Bless the Lord, O my soul! O Lord, my God, You are very great; You have clothed Yourself with majesty and glory. You cover with light like a garment, stretch out the heavens like a hanging." The garment of the tallit, then, is compared to a garment of light, and the tzitzit are compared to the heavens stretching and hanging downward.

The Talmud informs us that there are two worlds, the spiritual and the physical. For most of us, the physical world is reality and the spiritual world is ethereal and theoretical. For the mystic, though, spirituality is not only real, but it is true realism. Also, the notion of creation implies that this true reality existed before creation and is eternal, and creation of physicality lead to a derivative, new reality, by a process extending eternal reality to include also physical existence.

Thus, from a mystical perspective, the cloth of the tallit, the prayer shawl represents true reality; therefore it is substantial. Physical reality is less real, so it is represented by the area of non-cloth., by a void. From the perspective of the tallit, the created reality would be non-reality and nonexistence except for the tzitzit that stretch forth from real reality, extending reality also to the created realms. The notion of an intrinsic, spiritual reality which existed before creation, the Infinite Light, the realm of sephiros, (the Holy Emanations of the Infinite Light), and the souls of the righteous, all emanating from the Holy King, raises the question how this reality can have permitted extension to non-intrinsic creation. True, in the infinite potential which is part our understanding of the Ayn Sof, the Infinite, is also the possibility of created reality. However, that created reality does not reflect its source and therefore will not be emanated spontaneously into existence.

That is, intrinsic reality reflects its source in the sense expressed in recounting of creation in Genesis. After God emanated the light, the verse continues: "And it was evening, and it was morning, one day." The first day was not creation, strictly, in this sense, but rather emanation of light, where light reveals its source but adds nothing new. Therefore, it is called "one day", as Rashi, the major source of Biblical explanations, explains: "According to the order of expression used in this chapter, it should have said 'first day' as it is written for the other days: second, third, fourth. Why did it write 'one'? Because the Holy One, blessed be He, was alone in His world, for the angels were only created on the second day."

Thus, beginning creation proper on the second day, (it at least seemed that) the Holy One, blessed be He, was not alone in His world. This was the creation of a new, non-intrinsic reality in which other beings came into existence, but on the first day, the light emanated revealed that God alone exists. That light and realm are intrinsic. They reflect reality before something new is created. The verse refers to this level as as "You cover with light like a garment." That is, in the infinite potential of the Ayn Sof, there is the possibility of emanating what exists intrinsically in any case, and there is also the possibility of creating a new and different reality. We understand that these represent two distinctly different types of potential. On the level of potential, intrinsic reality exists already potentially, ready to be emanated, whereas created reality is in the realm of nonexistence until it is introduced ex nihilo.

The potential for intrinsic reality is represented by the tallit, and the potential for created reality by the empty space around the tallit. Moreover, the edge of the tallit separates them. That is, it is not in the nature of intrinsic, Godly reality to extend to created reality, nor is it in the nature of the created reality to attain the Godly. This is analogous to the division of the waters into upper and lower realms of the second day of creation.

The essence of mystical Judaism is that, although they should be connected, nevertheless, the intrinsic and created realms are connected. The question is how could this be possible? How could a new, separate and created reality issue from the intrinsic reality which simply reflects the Only One?

The letters of God's name provide the answer. Besides constituting a unity, as the verse states: "The Lord is One", each letter has its own individual signification.

The yud reflects intrinsic, eternal reality most purely. Analogous to what was described earlier, it does not extend down to the line, to the created reality of this world, but is separate from it, hovering above.

"The hai at the beginning of a word means "the". Whereas without "the", a noun is indefinite, the word "the" renders it definite and denoted. The hai makes the separateness and ungraspable character, itself, of the yud definite, and thereby, somewhat closer to the line, to created reality. Nevertheless, it represents the resolution of pure spirituality, and does not really extend to created being.

The vov means "and". it adds something to what was previously there. It is the true source of created reality in the Ayn Sof, denoting that the intrinsic reality of yud and hai can not contain the Infinite Light, which extends outward to create a new, non-intrinsic reality, too. Thus, unlike the yud, it extends down to the line, extending its souce in intrinsic reality even to created reality.

"Like the first hai, the second one renders the previous letter definite. Thus, just as the first hai represents the King, the yud, being on His throne, in the court and presence of His spiritual subjects, so the second hai represents the actual creation of a new reality through the extension of the Ayn Sof toward creation, represented by the vov.

That is, the vov links the intrinsic and created realities. How is it possible to connect a reality whose very nature is to be intrinsic and therefore separate, immutable and spiritual to a realm whose character is definite, new, and tends toward physicality and thus to transience?

The tallit provides us with the answer. The tallit represents a reality whose very nature is to be intrinsic and therefore separate, eternal, immutable and spiritual, and the edges represent the separateness of that reality. From that perspective, no new, created realm could ever exist. Moreover, it would seem impossible for two edges to come together, let alone to limit each other. After all, each edge is separate, eternal, immutable and spiritual in character. If, nevertheless, they do come together and do limit each other, it represents a domain well above and not contained by the intrinsic, eternal and immutable reality. This is the origin of the vov: the dimension of the Ayn Sof so infinite that it is not even contained by the intrinsic and eternal.

A corner of the tallit, then, represents the place or dimension of the infinite potential which is transcendent, which is not contained by the intrinsic and eternal, and extends even to what is new and created.

The corner of the tallit also represents orientation within the intrinsic realm toward the new reality beyond, toward creation. The (self-) limitation represented by the corner is a point, because in order to extend outside itself, outside the "one day", to the finite and created, it must begin with a definite point. For example, in order to

say something (creation was with God's speech) one must first know specifically what one wants, which is a single point. Afterwards the multiple details of what means to employ to get it, including speech, and then choice of words, can develop. It is curious that in order to extend beyond its intrinsic limits to the "outside", the Ayn Sof limits and turns away from itself. The expansion is achieved through contraction. As stated above, this limitation represents a level still higher than the reflection of the infinite in intrinsic reality. It is the origin of the "and", of the vov. The actual extension of reality to the new and created goes over the point of the corner of the tallit, but it is not the tallit (intrinsic realm) itself. Rather, the extension is by the fringe, the tzitzit. Thus, the actual fulfillment of the mitzvah, of the commandment, is through the fringe, which represents the actualization and complete expression of the vov. The mitzvahs are even higher than the eternal intrinsic realm, adding a still higher level to the intrinsic realm by extending the Ayn Sof beyond it.

Indeed, in Jewish mysticism the mitzvah of tzitzit is particularly connected to the letter vov. Thus the mystical book , the Tanya, states that he who omits tzitzit blemishes the letter vov of His name.

Although the tzitzit represent turning away from intrinsic spirituality toward the created world, they connect the two realms too. Connecting the two disparate realms is achieved by a balance which includes and accounts for each. This is represented by the corners of the tallit, which are a place which unite the tallit representing the eternal realm, and the non tallit, representing the created realm. The verse refers to this level as "stretch out the heavens like hanging."

This is further represented in the form of the tzitzit, which are strings tied and wrapped around each other for the first third of their length, then separate loose strings hanging down freely for the remaining two thirds. In the teachings of the saintly Ari za"l, the famous mystic, the first third represents the inner dimension. That is, the mystical realm is reflected in the knots and wraps of the first third of the length of the tzitzit, denoting the mystical meanings of the mitzvahs. There, the strings are attached to the tallit and intertwined, yet they extend downward: the separate elements of the new created reality are interwoven with the intrinsic, eternal realm. Departing from that level for the remaining two thirds of the tzitzit, the separate elements of reality evolve independently, each achieving its own separate connection to the new, created realm. By knowing and thinking about the significance of the mitzvah of tzitzit while performing the mitzvah, one is doing just what the tzitzit are supposed to do: to connect the inner, intrinsic, eternal realm to the new creation.

In the passage about tzitzit, the Torah states: "In order that you remember, and perform all of the commandments". From this the Rabbis derive that the commandment of tzitzit has the weight of all the other mitzvahs combined. That is, it has a general significance of which each other mitzvah partakes. Figuratively, each mitzvah is a fringe hanging at a corner of the tallit - of the eternal, intrinsic reality. The ideas behind tzitzit, linking eternity to the new creation through a series of spiritual levels and steps each of which are rooted in the intrinsic reality of "one day", a realm where only God exists, and simultaneously are oriented toward the physical creation, function in each mitzvah: they all serve to connect us

God. From http://www.jewishmag:com/BOMAG/tzitzit/tzitzit.htm
"<===|

# Talmudic Sources Concerning
# Prayer Shawls and Threads

## Legal Issues
Defining the term, "threads": Menachot 41b, 42a
Whether the commandment is person-based, or garment-based:
Shabbat 131a-b;
Menachot 41 a, 42b
Whether having threads on all of the four corners constitutes four
Separate commandments, or they are all necessary to fulfill a
single
commandment: Menachot 37b-38a
Not travelling 4 cubits without threads: Shabbat 118b
Doing the commandment with beautiful threads: Shabbat 133b
Whether Kohanim are obligated: Menachot 43a
Whether women are obligated: Succah 11a [See Rashi
"LePirzuma"]; Menachot 43a
Whether blind people are obligated: Menachot 43a
When minors become obligated: Succah 42a
Whether slaves wear them: Menachot 43a
Putting them on a corpse before burial: Menachot 41a
Requiring that one separate the threads: Menachot 42a
The threads are items of a commandment, not items of intrisic
holiness, and so may be disposed of after their use is finished:
Megillah 26b

## The Garment
The minimum size of such a garment: Menachot 40b-41a
Validity of threads for an undersized garment: Menachot 40b-41a
A borrowed garment: Menachot 44a

A garment which is entirely dyed blue: Menachot 38b, 41 b

A garment with 5 corners: Menachot 43b

A garment with 3 corners: Menachot 43b

Making wool threads for a garment of flax: Menachot 39a, 39b-40b

Making flax threads for a garment of wool: Menachot 39b

A garment of various types of silk: Menachot 39b

A nighttime garment: Menachot 40b, 41a, 46a

A garment which is stored in a box, where it is [not] intended for Eventual wearing: Menachot 41 a

A garment which has a corner, or some other part, made of leather: Menachot 40b

A garment which is currently folded in half, and not sewn up, partly sewn, or fully sewn: Menachot 41a

If the garment is torn, more or less than 3 finger-breadths from the corner: Menachot 41 a

Attaching a section of another garment to this one: Menachot 41 a

**The Threads**

Threading the dyed threads on the intermediate days of holidays, in an altered manner: Moed Katan 19a [2x]

Minimum/Maximum length of the threads: Menachot 41 b-42a

Using stolen threads: Succah 9a

Using threads which already extend, as loose threads, from the garment: Menachot 42b

Requiring that the threads be created with intent for use for the commandment: Succah 9a; Menachot 42b

Whether the material of the threads is determined by the material in the garment

["Min Kanaf"]: Menachot 38a, 38b, 39a, 39b

The validity of threads which are truncated, depending upon the size of the remainder: Menachot 38b, 39a, 41b

Using threads of wool and linen: Menachot 39b

Using threads which will create, with the garment, a mixture of wool and linen, in Jerusalem: Menachot 40a

## Blue Dye

Description of the snail from which the dye is taken: Menachot 44a

The snail from which the blue dye for threads is extracted, was found in Zevulun's portion in Israel: Megillah 6a

Definition of the color of blue dye: R. Berachot 9b "Techelet"

How the dye is processed: Menachot 42b

The dye's color, as reminiscent of the sea, which reminds of the heavens, which reminds of the Divine Throne: Menachot 43b

## The White Threads

Dyeing the "white" threads to be the same color as the garment: Menachot 41 b

The white as threads he holier threads: Menachot 39a [See Rashi]

Whether threads are valid without white threads: Menachot 38a-b

Whether white threads must precede the blue, or this is just the ideal format: Menachot 38a-b

It is worse to not have the white threads than to not have the blue-dyed threads, because the white threads are easier to get: Menachot 43b

## Making Threads

Whether one makes a blessing on making threads: Menachot 42a

Using threads which were connected to the garment beforehand: Succah 9a, 11a-b; Menachot 40b [2x]

Moving threads from one article of clothing to another: Pesachim 101a; Menachot 41a-b

Threads made by a gentile: Menachot 42a-b

Whether one may sell theads to a gentile, and why there should be a concern: Menachot 43a

Dyeing the blue thread with intent for the sake of the commandment: Eruvin 96b; Menachot 42b

## Wearing Threads

Making a blessing on each donning of threads: Menachot 43a

The Lord puts one who doesn't wear threads in ex-communication: Pesachim 113b

Reward for care in commandment of threads: Shabbat 118b

One should always be wearing threads: Shabbat 153a

Exemption of a merchant of threads from other commandments while engaged in marketing the threads: Succah 26a

Wearing invalid threads outside on Shabbat: Shabbat 139b; Menachot 37b-38a

# Christian Stola and the Prayer Shawl

The finer tallit, very likely, was similar in quality to the Roman pallium, and was worn only by distinguished men, rabbis, and scholars (B. B. 98a; Midrash Genesis Rabbah xxxvi.; Midrash Exodus Rabbah xxvii.). The tallit was sometimes worn partly doubled, and sometimes with the ends thrown over the shoulders

(Talmud references Shab. 147a; Men. 41a). The Episcopal churches also use a form of tallit in the form of stola. STOLE (Lat. stola and orarium, Fr. etole, It. stola, Sp. estola, Ger. Stola), a liturgical vestment of the Episcopal Churches, peculiar to the higher orders, i.e. deacons, priests and bishops.

## Roman Catholic Church

The Pallium is a circular band of white wool about two inches wide, with two pendants hanging down front and back. It is ornamented with six dark crosses of silk, and is worn over the liturgical vestments.

The pallium is made (at least partially) from the wool of lambs - suggesting Christ, the Lamb of God and the Good Shepherd - presented each year to the Pope on the feast of St. Agnes. Roman Catholic Church law requires a metropolitan to request the pallium from the Pope, either personally or by proxy, within three months of episcopal ordination or transfer. The pallium is worn only within the Archbishop's ecclesiastical province.

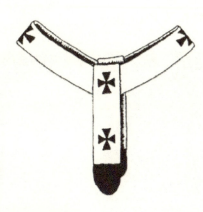

There are many theories as to the "ancestry" of the stole. Some say it came from the tallit (Jewish prayer mantle), because it is very similar to the present usage (as in the minister puts it on when he leads in prayer) but this theory is no longer regarded much today. More popular is the theory that the stole originated from a kind of liturgical napkin called an orarium very similar to the sudarium. In fact, in many places the stole is called the orarium. Therefore it is linked to the napkin used by Christ in washing the feet of his disciples, and is a fitting symbol of the yoke of Christ, the yoke of service.

## Eastern Churches

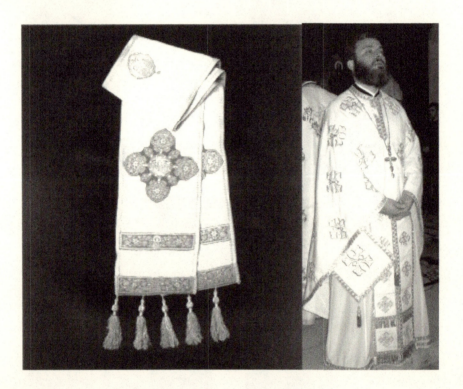

In the Eastern Orthodox and Eastern Catholic liturgical tradition, the omophorion (Greek:ou0<pop|ov ; Slavonic: omocbopb, omofor) is the distinguishing vestment of a bishop and the symbol of his spiritual and ecclesiastical authority. Originally of wool, it is a band of brocade decorated with crosses and is worn about the neck and around the shoulders.

# Omophorion

"Omophorion"--One of the bishop's vestments, made of a band of brocade worn about the neck and around the shoulders. It signifies the Good Shepherd by symbolizing the lost sheep that is found and thrown over the shoulders of the shepherd. The omophorion is a symbol of the spiritual authority of a bishop.

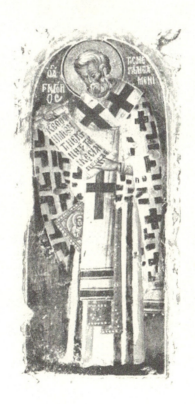

Fresco from 14th century depicting the omophorion

## Episcopalian Churches

The most likely origin for the stole, however, is to be connected with the scarf of office among Imperial officials in the Roman Empire. As members of the clergy became members of the Roman administration, they were granted certain honors, one specifically being a designator of rank within the imperial (and ecclesiastical) hierarchy. The various configurations of the stole (including the pallium or the omophorion) grew out of this usage. The original intent, then was to designate a person as belonging to a particular organization and to denote their rank within their group, a function which the stole continues to perform today. Thus, unlike other liturgical garments which were originally worn by every cleric or layman, the stole was a garment which was specifically restricted to particular classes of people based on occupation.